Tuscany travel guide 2024

The Ultimate Guide to Tuscany: Everything You Need to Know to Plan Your Trip

John Hendley

Table of contents

Introduction to Tuscany

Brimming with anticipation, Ethan eagerly embarked on a journey of a lifetime to Tuscany, his heart alight with wanderlust. He had acquired a captivating travel guide, aptly titled *"Tuscany travel guide,"* which had bewitched him at first glance. Its glossy cover showcased a mesmerizing Tuscan landscape, teasing his senses with promises of hidden treasures and unforgettable adventures.

As Ethan delved into the pages, he discovered a trove of invaluable information meticulously curated within its covers. With each turn of the well-worn pages, his excitement grew, mingling with gratitude for the travel guide that had become his trusted companion. The vivid descriptions transported him through time and space, introducing him to the vibrant culture, rich history, and breathtaking beauty of the Tuscan region.

The travel guide opened doors to the secrets of Tuscan cuisine, revealing the tantalizing flavors of locally produced fragrant olive oil, and delectable dishes that stirred the soul. Ethan reveled in the joy of savoring delicate bites of freshly baked bread, drizzled with golden Tuscan honey, while sipping velvety Chianti amidst the sprawling vineyards.

"Tuscany travel guide" also proved an invaluable source for discovering hidden gems. Armed with its well-researched suggestions, Ethan explored enchanting hilltop towns like San Gimignano, where medieval towers stood tall, whispering tales of ancient battles and lost love. He marveled at the ornate frescoes adorning the walls of the Basilica di Santa Maria Novella in Florence, their vivid hues echoing the passion of Renaissance masters.

Moreover, the travel guide introduced Ethan to the joys of Tuscan traditions and festivals. He found himself caught up in the infectious energy of the Palio di Siena, where horses thundered through the ancient streets, jockeys adorned in colorful regalia vying for victory. He danced to lively tarantellas at the Festa della Rificolona in Florence, twirling beneath a sea of paper lanterns, their warm glow casting a magical spell.

The guidebook acted as a beacon, guiding Ethan towards hidden trails that led him through the verdant Tuscan countryside. He discovered picturesque landscapes painted with vineyards, cypress-lined roads, and sunflower fields, all the while breathing in the sweet scent of Tuscan air and feeling the gentle caress of the warm Mediterranean breeze.

As Ethan's adventure came to a bittersweet close, he realized the profound impact the travel guide had on his journey. It had not only enriched his experiences but had also served as a guardian, ensuring he made the most of his time in Tuscany. The hidden corners, local haunts, and lesser-known wonders had all been unveiled, thanks to the book that had become his trusted ally.

With newfound wisdom and an overflowing heart, Ethan returned home, forever changed by his encounter with Tuscany's splendor. Inspired by his transformative journey, he vowed to share his experiences with fellow travelers, for he understood the immeasurable value of a well-crafted travel guide. A story whispered amidst the olive groves, its essence captured within the pages, reminding all who wander to embrace the gift of exploration and immerse themselves in the untold stories of the world.

And so, with a sense of deep fulfillment, Ethan began his own pilgrimage, not as a traveler, but as a storyteller, driven by the desire to inspire others to embark on their own odysseys, armed with a trusty guide to illuminate their path.

History of Tuscany

Tuscany, a region located in central Italy, has a rich and storied history that spans thousands of years. Its origins can be traced back to ancient times when it was inhabited by various Etruscan tribes, who left behind remarkable archaeological artifacts and tombs that still captivate historians today.

In the 4th century BCE, Tuscany came under Roman rule and flourished as part of the Roman Empire. The city of Florence, known as Florentia at the time, emerged as a significant center of commerce, art, and culture. The region enjoyed relative stability and prosperity under Roman governance.

After the fall of the Roman Empire, Tuscany faced a turbulent period marked by invasions from Germanic tribes and Lombards. It was during the Middle Ages that Tuscany witnessed the rise of powerful city-states, such as Florence, Pisa, Siena, and Lucca. These independent city-states competed for dominance, each cultivating its own unique cultural and artistic heritage.

Tuscany enjoyed a golden age of artistic and intellectual success during the Renaissance. The influential Medici family of Florence played a pivotal role in nurturing the arts and supporting renowned figures like Leonardo da Vinci, Michelangelo, and Botticelli. Florence became the epicenter of the Renaissance, attracting scholars, architects, and thinkers from across Europe.

In the 16th century, Tuscany came under the rule of the Medici Grand Duchy, transforming the region into a powerful political entity. The Medicis left an indelible mark on Tuscany, investing in infrastructure, trade, and education. Their patronage of the arts continued to flourish, fostering a climate of creativity that continues to shape the region's identity to this day.

The 19th century brought significant changes to Tuscany. After the fall of Napoleon, the region was briefly under the control of the Habsburg Empire before it became part of the unified Kingdom of Italy in 1861. Tuscany's cities experienced modernization and industrialization, and the region saw advancements in agriculture, commerce, and urban development.

Tuscany endured the challenges of the World Wars and played a role in the resistance against fascism during World War II. After the war, the region underwent reconstruction, preserving its historical and cultural heritage while adapting to the demands of the modern world.

Today, Tuscany stands as a beloved destination that blends the echoes of its ancient past with the vibrant pulse of the present. Its enchanting cities, picturesque landscapes, and renowned art treasures continue to attract visitors from around the globe. Tuscany remains a testament to the enduring legacy of human creativity, resilience, and the pursuit of beauty that has shaped its remarkable history.

Climate and Geography of Tuscany

Tuscany is a region located in central Italy, and it is widely known for its beautiful landscapes and cultural attractions. It has an overall Mediterranean climate, although it can vary slightly by the elevation and the proximity to the ocean. The coast has an average temperature of 27 °C (81 °F) in the summer, while it can drop to 10 °C (50 °F) in the winter. The interior regions of Tuscany have a warm and humid climate, with temperatures averaging between 15 and 20 °C (59 - 68 °F).

Tuscany is mainly composed of hills, and it has an average elevation of 500 meters (1640 feet). The highest peaks in the region are the Pratomagno at 1,752 meters (5760 ft.) and Mount Folonari at 1,470 meters (4824 ft.). The flat areas are located in the coastal regions, and they are the best suited for agriculture.

Tuscany is well traversed by numerous rivers and streams. The two biggest rivers are the Arno and Serchio, which give rise to the wide valleys in the Apennines. Tuscany's most fertile soils can be found in the coastal plains.

The landscape in Tuscany has been heavily shaped by its Mediterranean climate, and it is characterized by rolling hills, terraced vineyards, and beautiful cypress trees. The vineyards are some of the most well-known regions in Italy, and they produce some of the world's finest wines.

Tuscany has a rich and diverse set of geography that makes it one of the most visited regions in Italy. In addition to its beauty, the mild Mediterranean climate allows for a wide variety of activities and attractions available to visitors. The diverse landscape, from the rolling hills to the coastal plains to the mountain peaks, make it an ideal destination for nature lovers.

Whether one is looking for a quiet getaway or an active vacation, Tuscany offers something for everyone. From culture and landmarks to

outdoor activities and wine tasting, Tuscany
has it all.

Best Time to Visit Tuscany

Tuscany, located in central Italy, is a
picturesque region renowned for its stunning
landscapes, rich history, and exquisite cuisine.
With its charming countryside, vineyards, olive
groves, medieval towns, and iconic cities like
Florence, Siena, and Pisa, Tuscany attracts
visitors throughout the year. However, the best
time to visit Tuscany largely depends on your
preferences and what you want to experience
during your trip.

Spring (April to June) and fall (September to
October) are generally considered the best
seasons to visit Tuscany. These months offer
pleasant weather, with mild temperatures and
fewer crowds compared to the peak summer
season. Spring brings blooming flowers, lush
greenery, and vibrant landscapes, making it
ideal for outdoor activities such as hiking,
cycling, and exploring the countryside.
Additionally, this period is perfect for wine
enthusiasts as it coincides with the grape
harvest season, offering a chance to participate
in wine festivals and tastings.

In the fall, Tuscany's countryside transforms into a tapestry of warm colors as the vineyards and forests change with the season. The weather remains pleasant, allowing visitors to enjoy activities like wine tours, truffle hunting, and food festivals. Autumn is also a great time to visit Tuscany's art cities as they are less crowded, and you can explore renowned museums, cathedrals, and historic landmarks at a more relaxed pace.

The summer months (July and August) in Tuscany can be hot and crowded due to the influx of tourists. However, if you don't mind the higher temperatures and want to experience Tuscany's lively atmosphere, summer offers its own charm. The region comes alive with festivals, outdoor concerts, and cultural events. You can enjoy long evenings dining alfresco, savoring gelato, and exploring the vibrant streets of cities like Florence and Siena. It's advisable to book accommodations and attractions well in advance if you plan to visit during this peak season.

Winter (December to February) is considered the low season in Tuscany. The weather can be colder, especially in the hilly areas, and some tourist attractions may have reduced hours or be closed. However, if you're seeking a quieter and more affordable visit, winter can be a good time to explore Tuscany's cities and towns without the crowds. You can enjoy the Christmas markets, indulge in Tuscan cuisine, and experience the region's rich history and art in a more intimate setting.

In summary,the best time to visit Tuscany depends on your preferences. Spring and fall offer pleasant weather, blooming landscapes, and fewer crowds, while summer provides a lively and vibrant atmosphere. Winter is ideal for a quieter experience, albeit with colder temperatures. Whichever season you choose, Tuscany's timeless beauty and cultural treasures will leave you with unforgettable memories.

Safety and Security in Tuscany.

Tuscany, like most tourist destinations in Italy, is generally a safe region for visitors. However, it's important to be aware of certain safety and security considerations to ensure a smooth and enjoyable trip. Here are some key points to keep in mind when it comes to safety and security in Tuscany:

General Safety Precautions: Tuscany is considered a safe destination, but it's always wise to take basic safety precautions. Keep an eye on your personal belongings, especially in crowded tourist areas, and be cautious of pickpockets. Avoid displaying valuable items openly and use hotel safes to store passports, cash, and other important documents.

Transportation Safety: Tuscany has a well-developed transportation system, including trains, buses, and taxis, which are generally safe to use. However, it's recommended to be cautious when using public transportation during busy periods and to keep an eye on your belongings. If you rent a car, make sure to follow traffic rules and be aware of any local driving customs.

Scams and Tourist Traps: Like in any popular tourist destination, there might be scams or tourist traps targeting visitors. Be cautious of individuals offering unsolicited assistance, such as helping with your luggage or providing tours, as they may expect payment in return. It's advisable to book tours and activities through reputable companies or your hotel concierge.

Health and Medical Services: Tuscany has good healthcare facilities and services, both public and private. If you require medical assistance, hospitals and clinics can provide quality care. It's recommended to have travel insurance that covers any medical expenses and to carry a list of emergency contact numbers.

Emergency Services: In case of an emergency, the emergency number in Italy is 112. It connects you to police, ambulance services, and the fire department. Be prepared to provide your location and a clear description of the situation when making an emergency call.

Natural Hazards: Tuscany is prone to natural hazards such as wildfires, especially during the hot and dry summer months. Pay attention to local news and follow any instructions or warnings from authorities. If you plan to hike or explore rural areas, inform someone about your plans and consider hiring a local guide for safety and navigation.

COVID-19 Safety: During the ongoing COVID-19 pandemic, it's crucial to stay updated on the latest travel restrictions, guidelines, and health protocols implemented by the Italian government and local authorities.

Follow recommended safety measures such as wearing masks, practicing social distancing, and maintaining good hand hygiene.

It's important to note that while Tuscany is generally safe, it's always prudent to exercise caution and stay informed about the local conditions and any travel advisories before your trip. By staying alert and taking basic safety precautions, you can have a wonderful and secure experience exploring the beautiful region of Tuscany.

Chapter 1

Practical Information

Currency and Exchange

The currency of Italy is the euro (EUR). The exchange rate in 2024, is 1 EUR = 1.07 USD.

There are a few ways to exchange currency in Tuscany. You can exchange your currency at a bank, a currency exchange bureau, or an ATM.

Banks usually offer the best exchange rates, but they may have limited hours and may not be located in convenient places. Currency exchange bureaus are more common and have more flexible hours, but they may charge a commission. ATMs are the most convenient option, but they may not offer the best exchange rates.

If you are planning on using your credit or debit card in Tuscany, it is a good idea to let your bank know that you will be traveling there. This will help to prevent your card from being blocked due to suspicious activity.

Here are some tips for exchanging currency in Tuscany:

- Before leaving, do some research and check the exchange rates.
- A credit or debit card without a foreign transaction fee is something to think about using.
- Avoid exchanging currency at the airport or train station, as these places often have the worst exchange rates.
- Be sure to check the commission fees charged by currency exchange bureaus.

Here are some currency exchange services located in Tuscany:

- Money Exchange Office Fratelli Barsanti Tommaso and Francesco and c. s.n.c.
- Change Italia
- Change Exchange Marco Alunno

Language and Communication

The official language of Tuscany is Italian, which is also the national language of Italy.

However, there is a regional dialect of Italian called Tuscan, which is spoken by many people in the region. Tuscan is considered to be the foundation of modern Italian, and many of the words and phrases used in Italian today come from Tuscan.

If you are planning on visiting Tuscany, it is a good idea to learn a few basic phrases in Italian or Tuscan. Your journey will be more pleasurable, and you'll be able to converse with the locals thanks to this.

Here are a few common phrases that you might find useful:

- Ciao: Hello
- Arrivederci: Goodbye
- Per favore: Please
- Grazie: Thank you
- Mi scusi: Excuse me
- Dove è il bagno?: Where is the bathroom?
- Quanto costa?: How much does it cost?
- Non capisco: I don't understand
- Parli inglese?: Do you speak English?

If you are not able to learn any Italian or Tuscan before your trip, don't worry. Most people in Tuscany will be able to understand basic English. However, it is always appreciated when you make an effort to speak the local language.

Here are a few tips for communicating in Tuscany:

- Be patient. The locals may not speak English as well as you think they do.
- Be polite. Use please and thank you, even if you are not sure if the person understands you.
- Use simple language. Avoid using slang or complex sentences.
- Point and gesture. This can be helpful if you are trying to communicate something that you don't know the word for.

Local Customs and Etiquette

Here are some local customs and etiquette in Tuscany that you should know about when visiting:

- Greetings: When greeting someone in Tuscany, it is customary to shake hands and say "buongiorno" (good morning) or "buonasera" (good evening). If you are meeting someone for the first time, you may also want to say "piacere" (nice to meet you).

- Politeness: Italians are very polite people, so it is important to be polite when you are visiting Tuscany. This means using please and thank you, and being respectful of other people's space.
- Dining: When dining in Tuscany, it is customary to wait for everyone to be served before starting to eat. It is also considered polite to finish all of the food on your plate.
- Tipping: Tipping is not expected in Tuscany, but it is appreciated. If you do decide to tip, a small amount is sufficient.
- Public displays of affection: Public displays of affection are not as common in Tuscany as they are in some other countries. It is generally considered polite to keep your displays of affection to a minimum in public.
- Photography: It is generally considered polite to ask permission before taking someone's photo. This is especially important if you are taking photos of people in religious or historical sites.

Here are some additional tips for following local customs and etiquette in Tuscany:

- Dress modestly: When visiting religious or historical sites, it is important to dress modestly. This entails covering your legs and shoulders.
- Be aware of your surroundings: Tuscany is a beautiful region, but it is also a popular tourist destination. Be aware of your surroundings and take precautions to keep yourself safe.
- Be respectful of the culture: Tuscany is a rich and diverse region with a long history. Be respectful of the culture and customs of the people who live there.

By following these tips, you can ensure that you have a respectful and enjoyable visit to Tuscany.

Emergency Contacts

Here are some emergency contacts in Tuscany that you should know about:

★ Emergency number: 112
★ State Police (Polizia di Stato): 113
★ Fire Department (Vigili del fuoco): 115
★ Finance Police (Guardia di finanza): 117
★ Emergency medical services: 118
★ Women Abuse: 055 427 7493
★ Italian Red Cross Ambulance Service: 055 215 381
★ Anti-Poison (Centro Antiveleni): 055 427 7238
★ Emergency Vet: 800 029 449

You can also call the Tourist Assistance Service (Servizio Assistenza Turistica) for help with any travel-related emergencies. The number is 116 000.

If you are calling from a mobile phone, you may need to dial 0039 before the emergency number.

It is important to remember that these are just some of the emergency contacts in Tuscany. There may be other numbers that you need to call depending on the situation.

Here are some tips for calling emergency services in Tuscany:

- Stay calm and speak clearly.
- Inform the operator of your location and the emergency's details.
- Follow the operator's instructions.
- If you are calling from a mobile phone, be sure to turn on your location services so that the operator can find you.

Chapter 2

Top Attractions and Places to Visit in Tuscany

Florence

Florence is a top tourist destination in Tuscany, and for good reason. The city is home to some of the most famous works of Renaissance art and architecture in the world, including Michelangelo's David, Botticelli's Birth of Venus, and the Duomo.

In addition to its art and architecture, Florence also has a vibrant cultural scene. There are many museums, theaters, and opera houses in the city, and there are always something going on. Whether you're interested in art, history, or culture, Florence is a great place to visit.

Here are some of the top attractions in Florence:

- Duomo: The Duomo is the main cathedral in Florence, and it's one of the most iconic buildings in the city. The cathedral has a terracotta-tiled dome that was engineered by Brunelleschi, and it's one of the most impressive feats of engineering in the Renaissance.
- Galleria dell'Accademia: The Galleria dell'Accademia is home to Michelangelo's David, one of the most famous sculptures in the world. The statue is a must-see for any visitor to Florence.
- Uffizi Gallery: One of the most renowned art galleries in the entire world is the Uffizi Gallery. The museum houses a collection of Renaissance art, including works by Botticelli, da Vinci, and Raphael.
- Piazza della Signoria: Piazza della Signoria is the main square in Florence. The square is home to the Palazzo

Vecchio, the seat of the Florentine government, and the Loggia dei Lanzi, a loggia that houses a collection of sculptures.

- Ponte Vecchio: Florence's Ponte Vecchio bridge crosses the Arno River.The bridge is lined with shops and jewelers, and it's one of the most popular tourist destinations in the city.

Siena

Siena is a beautiful city in Tuscany, Italy, and is a UNESCO World Heritage Site. It is known for its medieval architecture, including the Piazza del Campo, the Duomo, and the Torre del Mangia. Siena is also home to the Palio di Siena, a horse race that takes place twice a year.

Here are some of the top attractions in Siena:

- Piazza del Campo: This is the main square in Siena and is a UNESCO World Heritage Site. It is a beautiful square with a shell-shaped shape and is surrounded by many important buildings, including the Palazzo Pubblico and the Torre del Mangia.
- Duomo: The Duomo is the cathedral of Siena and is one of the most important examples of Gothic architecture in Italy. It is a beautiful building with a facade that is decorated with sculptures and mosaics.
- Torre del Mangia: This is the bell tower of the Palazzo Pubblico and is one of the tallest buildings in Siena. It offers breathtaking city views.
- Palio di Siena: This is a horse race that takes place twice a year in Piazza del Campo. It is a very popular event and is a great way to experience the culture of Siena.
- Santa Maria della Scala: This is a complex of buildings that includes a hospital, a museum, and a library. It is a UNESCO World Heritage Site and is a

great place to learn about the history of Siena.

- Battistero di San Giovanni: This is the baptistery of Siena and is a beautiful building with a white marble facade. It is a great place to see some of the best examples of Sienese art.

Siena is a great place to visit if you are interested in history, art, and culture. It is a beautiful city with a lot to offer visitors.

Here are some other things to do in Siena:
- Visit the Pinacoteca Nazionale, which houses a collection of Sienese art.
- Consider enrolling in a culinary class to learn how to prepare typical Tuscan cuisine.
- Go wine tasting in the surrounding Chianti region.
- Hike or bike in the hills surrounding Siena.
- Visit the town of San Gimignano, which is a short drive from Siena.

Lucca

Lucca is a beautiful city in Tuscany, Italy, that is known for its well-preserved Renaissance walls, its charming Piazza Anfiteatro, and its many historical churches and palaces. It is a well-liked vacation spot, and for good reason. There are many things to see and do in Lucca, from exploring the city's historic center to hiking or biking along the walls.

Here are some of the top attractions in Lucca:

- The Walls of Lucca: These massive walls were built in the 16th century and are now a UNESCO World Heritage Site. You can walk or bike along the top of the walls for stunning views of the city and the surrounding countryside.

- Piazza Anfiteatro: This charming square was once the site of a Roman amphitheater. Today, it is a popular spot for locals and tourists alike to relax, people-watch, and enjoy a coffee or gelato.
- Duomo di Lucca: This beautiful cathedral is the most important religious building in Lucca. It was built in the 12th century and features a Gothic interior and a Renaissance exterior.
- Torre Guinigi: This 40-meter-tall tower is one of the most recognizable landmarks in Lucca. It provides sweeping views of both the city and the countryside beyond.
- Basilica di San Frediano: This 12th-century church is one of the oldest in Lucca. It features a beautiful Romanesque facade and a Gothic interior.
- Palazzo Pfanner: This elegant palace was built in the 18th century. It features a beautiful garden with fountains, statues, and a gazebo.

Lucca is a charming city with a lot to offer visitors. Whether you're interested in history, architecture, or simply relaxing in a beautiful setting, Lucca is a great place to visit.

Here are some additional tips for visiting Lucca:

- The best time to visit Lucca is during the spring or fall, when the weather is mild.
- If you're planning on visiting the Walls of Lucca, be sure to wear comfortable shoes.
- There are many great restaurants in Lucca, so you're sure to find something to your taste.
- If you're interested in learning more about Lucca's history, be sure to visit the Museo Civico.

San Gimignano

San Gimignano is a beautiful medieval town in Tuscany, Italy. It is known for its 14 soaring towers, which earned it the nickname "Manhattan of the Middle Ages." The town is also home to a number of other historical and cultural attractions, including the Collegiata di Santa Maria Assunta, the Town Hall, and the Civic Museum.

San Gimignano is a popular tourist destination, and it is easy to see why. The town is absolutely stunning, and it is a great place to wander around and explore. There are also a number of excellent restaurants and shops in San Gimignano, so you can easily spend a day or two enjoying everything the town has to offer.

The following are some of the top activities in San Gimignano:
- Visit the 14 towers: This is a must-do for any visitor to San Gimignano. The towers are a symbol of the town's wealth and power in the Middle Ages, and they offer stunning views of the surrounding countryside.
- Explore the historic center: The historic center of San Gimignano is a UNESCO World Heritage Site. It is a maze of

narrow streets and alleyways, lined with medieval buildings.

- Visit the Collegiata di Santa Maria Assunta: This church is one of the most important in Tuscany. It is home to a number of beautiful frescoes, including the "Madonna with Child" by Lippo Memmi.
- Take a walk on the walls: The walls of San Gimignano offer stunning views of the town and the surrounding countryside. You can walk along the walls for about 2 kilometers.
- Visit the Civic Museum: This museum houses a collection of art and artifacts from the Middle Ages and Renaissance.
- Enjoy the food and wine: San Gimignano is home to some excellent restaurants and wineries. Make sure to sample some of the regional favorites, including Vernaccia wine and pici pasta.

San Gimignano is a truly magical place, and it is a must-visit for any traveler to Tuscany.

Chianti

Chianti is a wine region in Tuscany, Italy, that is famous for its Chianti Classico wine. The region is located between the cities of Florence and Siena, and is known for its rolling hills, vineyards, and medieval villages.

Some of the most popular tourist destinations in Chianti include:

- Greve in Chianti: The main town in the Chianti Classico region, Greve is home to a number of wineries, as well as the Chianti Classico Museum.
- Castellina in Chianti: A hilltop town with a well-preserved medieval center, Castellina is a great place to wander around and explore the local shops and restaurants.

- Radda in Chianti: A small town with a charming main square, Radda is a great place to sample some of the local wines.
- San Donato in Poggio: A hilltop town with panoramic views of the surrounding countryside, San Donato is a great place to relax and enjoy the peace and quiet.
- Volpaia: A medieval village that is now a popular tourist destination, Volpaia is a great place to experience the traditional Tuscan way of life.

In addition to its wine and scenery, Chianti also offers a variety of other activities, such as hiking, biking, and horseback riding. The region is also home to a number of castles and churches, which are worth visiting for their historical and architectural significance.

If you are looking for a beautiful and relaxing place to visit in Tuscany, Chianti is a great option. With its stunning scenery, delicious wine, and charming villages, Chianti is sure to leave you with lasting memories.

Here are some tips for visiting Chianti:

- The best time to visit Chianti is during the spring or fall, when the weather is mild.
- If you are interested in wine, be sure to book a wine tasting at one of the many wineries in the region.
- If you are looking for a more active vacation, be sure to bring your hiking boots or bike.
- No matter what your interests are, you are sure to find something to enjoy in Chianti.

Chapter 3

Accommodation

Hotels in Tuscany

Here are some hotels in Tuscany with current prices:

Hotel Da Vinci in Montecatini Terme is a 4-star hotel with a rooftop pool and restaurant.

Notti Etrusche a Sovana in Sovana is a 3-star bed and breakfast with Etruscan ruins nearby.

B&B Hotel Arezzo in Arezzo is a 3-star hotel with free Wi-Fi and breakfast buffet.

Relais Il Chiostro di Pienza in Pienza is a 4-star hotel in a 13th-century convent.

Albergo Ristorante Miramonti in Consuma is a 3-star hotel with mountain views and a restaurant.

These are just a few examples of hotels in Tuscany. There are many other hotels to choose from, with a wide range of prices to fit your budget.

When booking a hotel in Tuscany, it is important to consider the following factors:

- Location: Where do you want to stay? In a city, town, or village? Near the beach, mountains, or countryside?
- Price: How much are you willing to spend on your hotel stay?
- Amenities: What amenities are important to you? A pool, free Wi-Fi, breakfast included?
- Reviews: Read reviews from other guests to get an idea of what to expect from your hotel stay.

Chapter 5

Getting Around

Public Transportation in Tuscany

Sure. Here is some information about public transportation in Tuscany:

Trains: Tuscany has a well-developed train network, with trains connecting all of the major cities and many of the smaller towns. The fastest trains are the Frecciarossa (red arrow) trains, which can reach speeds of up to 300 km/h. Other types of trains include the Intercity (IC) trains, the Regionale (R) trains, and the Treno regionale (TR) trains.

Buses: There are also a number of bus companies that operate in Tuscany, providing connections between cities, towns, and villages. The main bus company is Autolinee Toscane, which operates a fleet of over 1,000 buses. Other bus companies include Copit, BluBus, and Vai Bus.

City buses: All of the major cities in Tuscany have their own city bus system. These buses are a convenient way to get around the city center and to some of the surrounding areas.

Taxis: Taxis are also available in all of the major cities in Tuscany. They can be a convenient way to get around, but they can be expensive.

The best way to get around Tuscany depends on your budget and your travel plans. If you are on a tight budget, buses are a good option. If you are looking for a more comfortable and faster way to travel, trains are a good option. And if you are looking for a way to get to some of the smaller towns and villages, taxis or city buses may be your best option.

Here are some tips for using public transportation in Tuscany:

- Buy your tickets in advance: If you are traveling by train, you can buy your tickets online or at the train station. If you are traveling by bus, you can buy your tickets at the bus station or on the bus.

- Validate your tickets: Once you have your ticket, you need to validate it in the machine at the train station or bus stop.
- Be aware of the timetables: Make sure you know the timetables for the trains or buses you are taking. This will help you avoid delays.
- Be prepared for delays: Public transportation in Tuscany can be subject to delays, especially during peak travel times. Be prepared for this and allow extra time for your journey.

Car Rental in Tuscany

Sure. Here is some information about car rental in Tuscany:

Rental car companies: There are many different rental car companies operating in Tuscany, including Avis, Budget, Europcar, Hertz, and Sixt. You can find these companies at the airports, train stations, and in major cities and towns.

Prices: Car rental prices in Tuscany vary depending on the time of year, the type of car you rent, and the rental company you choose.

In general, you can expect to pay between €30 and €100 per day for a rental car.

Documents: When you rent a car in Tuscany, you will need to present your driver's license, passport, and credit card. You may also need to pay a security deposit.

Insurance: It is important to purchase insurance when you rent a car in Tuscany. You'll be safeguarded by this in the event of an incident or theft. Your specific situation will determine the kind of insurance you require.

Driving in Tuscany: The roads in Tuscany are generally good, but there can be traffic, especially in the cities. You should also be aware of the speed limits, which are lower than in some other countries.

Here are some tips for renting a car in Tuscany:
- Book your car in advance: This is especially important during peak travel times.
- Compare prices from different rental companies: You can use a website like Kayak or Expedia to compare prices from different companies.

- Read the terms and conditions carefully: Make sure you understand what is covered by the insurance before you rent the car.
- Be aware of the fuel policy: Some rental companies charge extra for fuel, so make sure you know what the policy is before you start your rental.

Shopping and Dining in Tuscany

Here are some specific places to visit for shopping and dining in Tuscany:

Shopping
- **Leather Market in Florence:** This is a must-visit for anyone interested in leather goods. You'll find everything from wallets and bags to shoes and belts
- **Antique Market in Arezzo:** This market is held every Sunday and is a great place to find antiques, collectibles, and other treasures.
- **Art Galleries in Siena:** Siena is home to a number of art galleries, including the Pinacoteca Nazionale di Siena and the Museo Civico.

Dining

- **Trattoria Il Latini:** This restaurant in Florence is a great place to try traditional Tuscan dishes. The pasta is made fresh daily and the service is excellent.
- **Enoteca Pinchiorri:** This Michelin-starred restaurant in Florence is a must-visit for foodies. The tasting menu is a true culinary experience.
- **Osteria del Cinghiale Bianco:** This restaurant in Montepulciano is a great place to try the local cuisine. The pici pasta is a must-try.

Bonus

Tips for Visiting Tuscany

Tuscany is a beautiful region in Italy that is known for its stunning scenery, delicious food, and rich history. If you are planning a trip to Tuscany, here are some professional tips to help you make the most of your visit:

Plan your trip in advance: Tuscany is a popular tourist destination, so it is important to plan your trip in advance, especially if you are traveling during peak season. Book your flights and accommodations early, and research the different places you want to visit.

Choose the right time of year to visit: Tuscany has a mild climate, so you can visit any time of year. However, the best time to visit is during the spring (April-June) or fall (September-October) when the weather is warm but not too hot.

Get around easily: Tuscany is a relatively small region, so it is easy to get around by train, bus, or car. If you are planning on doing a lot of sightseeing, I recommend renting a car.

Stay in a charming town: Tuscany is home to many charming towns, each with its own unique character. Some of my favorite towns include Florence, Siena, San Gimignano, and Montepulciano.

Visit the major cities: Tuscany is home to some of Italy's most famous cities, including Florence, Siena, and Pisa. These cities are home to world-renowned art, architecture, and history.

Explore the countryside: Tuscany is also home to stunning countryside, with rolling hills, vineyards, and olive groves. Be sure to take some time to explore the countryside and enjoy the beautiful scenery.

Taste the local food: Tuscany is known for its delicious food, so be sure to try some of the local dishes. Some of my favorites include Bistecca alla Fiorentina, Pappa al pomodoro, and Ribollita.

Learn about the history: Tuscany has a rich history, so be sure to visit some of the historical sites, such as the Leaning Tower of Pisa and the Piazza del Campo in Siena.

Conclusion

In conclusion, "Tuscany Travel Guide" serves as an invaluable resource for travelers seeking to explore the captivating region of Tuscany. Throughout this book, we have embarked on a journey that has uncovered the timeless beauty, rich history, and cultural wonders that define this remarkable destination.

By delving into the chapters, readers have gained a comprehensive understanding of Tuscany's diverse landscapes, from the rolling hills of Chianti to the picturesque vineyards of Montalcino. We have explored the iconic cities of Florence, Siena, and Pisa, marveling at their architectural marvels, renowned museums, and artistic treasures.

Beyond its physical allure, this guide sheds light on the profound cultural legacy that defines Tuscany. The Renaissance era, with its groundbreaking art and intellectual achievements, has been explored in depth, revealing the profound impact of luminaries such as Leonardo da Vinci and Michelangelo.

Furthermore, "Tuscany Travel Guide" has offered practical advice and useful tips, guiding travelers through the region's transportation systems, accommodations, and local customs. Whether navigating the narrow streets of medieval towns or engaging with the warm and hospitable locals, readers have been equipped with the tools necessary to make their visit to Tuscany an unforgettable experience.

In summary, "Tuscany Travel Guide" is a comprehensive compendium that captures the essence of this extraordinary region. Its meticulously researched information, coupled with vivid descriptions and stunning visuals, has successfully ignited wanderlust and provided travelers with the knowledge and inspiration needed to embark on their own Tuscany adventure. As readers close this book, they are left with a deep appreciation for Tuscany's beauty, heritage, and the countless treasures it has to offer.

Made in the USA
Monee, IL
02 January 2025

75800615R00036